THE GHOSTS OF LOST ANIMALS

Praise for The Ghosts of Lost Animals

In her wonderful new collection *The Ghosts of Lost Animals*, Michelle Bonczek Evory weaves magic with sensuality, intelligence with animal hunger, cynicism with wonder. Her work will remind you of the work of many other poets, and also of nobody else. When I first started reading these poems, I thought: love child of Russell Edson and Kim Addonizio, but then that didn't seem quite right. The book seems to miraculously teeter between the passion that drives these poems and the discerning critical eye that keeps them tethered to the page. Reading this book is like eating a multi-course meal where each bite surprises, delights and satisfies.

—Beth Gylys

Also from Gunpowder Press:
The Tarnation of Faust: Poems by David Case
Mouth & Fruit: Poems by Chryss Yost
Shaping Water: Poems by Barry Spacks
Original Face: Poems by Jim Peterson
Instead of Sadness: Poems by Catherine Abbey Hodges
What Breathes Us: Santa Barbara Poets Laureate, 2005-2015
Edited by David Starkey
Burning Down Disneyland: Poems by Kurt Olsson
Unfinished City: Poems by Nan Cohen
Raft of Days: Poems by Catherine Abbey Hodges
Posthumous Noon: Poems by Aaron Baker

Shoreline Voices Projects:
Buzz: Poets Respond to SWARM
Edited by Nancy Gifford and Chryss Yost
Rare Feathers: Poems on Birds & Art
Edited by Nancy Gifford, Chryss Yost, and George Yatchisin
To Give Life a Shape: Poems Inspired by the Santa Barbara Museum of Art
Edited by David Starkey and Chryss Yost

The Ghosts of Lost Animals

Poems

Michelle Bonczek Evory

Gunpowder Press • Santa Barbara
2019

Published by Gunpowder Press
David Starkey, Editor
PO Box 60035
Santa Barbara, CA 93160-0035

Cover image: "Always Searching" by Donald R. Miller
Author Photo: Robert Evory

ISBN-13: 978-0-9986458-4-1

www.gunpowderpress.com

For Rob

ACKNOWLEDGEMENTS

Thank you to the journals below for giving many of these poems their first home.

Adanna: "Love,"

Apercus Quarterly: "The Cardinal"

Connotations Press: "The Return"

Crazyhorse: "19-19"

Cream City Review: "Where I Turn Bad"

The Fertile Source: "The Courtyard"

Green Mountains Review: "Artery," "Embrace," "Fatness," "Fetus," "Theories of Relativity"

James Dickey Review: "Love Poem"

Margie: "Failed Attempt"

Midwest Quarterly Review: "Poem from the Coast"

New York Quarterly: "Alarm"

Orion Magazine: "Before Fort Clatsop," "Advection, Nova Scotia"

The Progressive: "Absolution"

The Seneca Review: "Pastoral"

Spillway: "Song"

Stone Canoe: "Burial Grounds"

Terminus: "Meal"

Wasafiri: International Contemporary Writing: "Miniature Museum, Prague"

Water~Stone: "The Afterlife of Pennies," "Four Corners"

Weber—The Contemporary West: "Yaquina Bay, and Darkness"

Poems have also appeared or are forthcoming in the following collections:

"Artery" appears in *Meridian Anthology of Contemporary Poetry. Vol. VII.*

"Burial Grounds" appears in *New Millennium Writings 2014.*

"Chico Hot Springs Saloon, MT" appears in *Manifest West: Even Cowboys Carry Cellphones.*

"Four Corners" received the 2007 John Woods Prize in poetry and the 2009 Jane Kenyon Award in poetry.

"Entering the Body" appears in *Best New Poets* 2013.

"Honeymoon" was published as a broadside by Architrave Press.

"Wooded Road, Lake Superior" is forthcoming in *Amethyst and Agate: Poems of Lake Superior.*

"Yaquina Bay, and Darkness" received the Dr. Sherwin W. Howard **Award** for poetry in 2011.

Some of these poems appear in the chapbook *The Art of the Nipple* published by Orange Monkey Publishing.

NOTE

In the poem "Burial Grounds," the line "Whoever finds us will think we were a small, stupid people" is from Alex Lemon.

Contents

III.

I.

Artery

What will they find when they cut you open?
Who will be there when they take back your ribs
and press onward to your heart? Will they see me
kneeling at the edge of your river of blood?
Will there be earlier versions of you? Of us
floating by in a rowboat full of moonlight?
Will they see your mother or your father
or how you imagined they could have been?
Will they be able to see the face of your own
child? Or will they have to cut me open for that?
What if there are stars in your veins? Or goldfish?
Or gold? Will they choose to keep hidden those things
you hide too well? How can they tell?
What if, in a quest for your heart, they find
no heart? Find that someone had already been there
and stolen it? What if it is there and they open it and they see
another heart inside? What if they cut that heart open
and find another heart inside that one? What if the hearts we carry
belong to someone else? Would you want yours back?
What if they told you, after they were done,
upon your waking, that your heart is not a heart
but a star, pulsing and ready to fall? And that pieces of hearts
have been falling like meteors into other hearts
this entire time? Would your heart be cratered like the moon?
Or smooth like a tumbled stone? What if
your heart is a planet where if you look closely
you can see grasslands and wings? Have I told you,
when it is quiet, to the beat of your body,
I hear my own voice singing?

Aria

I am reading this to you from a stage,
from a bathtub full of mineral salt, from a canoe

lost in the Pacific like a paperclip
holding a death certificate. I am reading this from a drop

of water, a sand speck sunk
to the bottom, a little island dome.

We are on Jupiter's smallest moon, in a poppy,
in a bean field. We are sunflowers and a herd of cows.

This is a field of vision. It grew long before me, before
you. Before I walked for the last time

to the rail of my grandfather's bed, away
for the first time from the rail of my daughter's crib.

I am reading this like it is the last thing I will read.
I am reading this like it is the only thing you will hear.

Light through paper before the smoke, four lives
in a four-wheel truck on a Baghdad roadside.

You can smell the metal, the sap, the blood.
You can hear my voice saying *your son*.

I am reading this to you under a veil in Sudan,
as we lay beside one another on the shores of Normandy,

from behind the crosshairs of a gun, from a corner, blind-
folded, hands bound.

Words are rising to a sky over Moscow, Krakow,
Tikrit, New York, Hiroshima, Berlin. Sounds are moving

like waves toward Japan. I am holding this page
like a scroll, untying the string. I am folding my words

into an airplane, into a passenger pigeon. I am reading loudly,
softly, silently to myself. I am singing

from the hospital where your grandfather met
your grandmother, from the dance floor where your mother met

your father, from the corner where you will meet me.
You are holding the hand of someone

you do not remember, whose tongue catches
snow under clouds full of planes, full of men full of light.

I am reading you wind
through which these bodies will fall. I am the net

on which they will land. Here are their eyes, their feet,
their blood. Here are their voices. Open your hands.

Entering the Body

after Gunter von Hagen's Body Worlds

All I could think of at first
was cooking. Of that skinned

rabbit in my freezer, fur torn, gaze
jammed between a package of phyllo

and a carton of ice cream.
Of all that succulent meat

dripping from its own skeleton,
sweet marrow and a bottle of merlot, but

even here
I end up in the palace of longing.

Caught in the arms of no arms.
Trying to bend a body

to my own. A skeleton
follows its muscled canvas

and I long
to be inside one, to hold
the other.

But you can't translate flesh.

Not with polymer, nor contemplation,
not even with a prolonged hand

shake or make out session.
Not in the slow unbuttoning

of a wine-stained blouse or in the stripping
of tendon from bone, muscle filleted

into C-section, pelvis cavity unsewn.
In this case, a uterus

the size of a thumb. Inside me, one jabs
like an eyelash in the heavens (yes,

the heavens). Here in this museum,
two blue eyes drift from two halves

of a severed head. How long do we stare
into mirrors. So long, I know,

my eyes roll
from their pockets till they bump
my tiny

tiny ossicles dripping notes
into my ears, *not yet*
not yet.

But flesh will not wait.
I want to wrap my arms around this

sculpture's waist and ask him, *anything?*
Nuzzle my chin in the meat-cleave

of his shoulder. Play my fingers
over his bones, over his exposed

vertebrae like a vibraphone.
Lick his neck until his brain coral

flowers.

Where I Turn Bad

I start thinking of flammable material, the kind
        we buy cheap from India
                but then I remember my grandfather's story
about a chapel carved out of salt. White steeple, white
        door, white people. We've been here way too long.
                So when the light changes, I speed
        until you and I glide
                over the freshly laid road, the smooth road
we fucked into existence, only you
        are not in the car and the white line that splits
the road in half reminds me of how
        we cannot live without salt. But this all has to do
                with the road. I light a cigarette, change
the subject, only I do not have cigarettes
        and don't smoke. The road is black
                like someone else's lungs. The cilia grow
hard, like art, from the tar. Sculptures, scars, bread. The road.
        The turn I made at the light is illegal. But it's the one
                that brought me
to you. I'm illegal not because I'm too young
        or because I'm a virgin in some country
                where virginity is collateral for land, or wine,
or salt, a country in which you are not a king or a pirate
        washed ashore a beach whose shells tongue your ear
                when you're not listening.
You don't kiss me because of this,
        only you do and I like it and I kiss you back, which is how
                we get the road. The smooth one. A story

about our lips and our legs entwining like jelly forms.
        My tongue licks your salt
                like a deer. *Shhh*. I'd be hunted and stoned to death
should they hear, as this culture is not one
        in which this would happen, but one in which a woman
                can be arrested for carrying too many
vibrators on a Texas highway. Good thing
        I took the one out of the glove box. Pass the bread. Here, I offer you
                my wrist, soft as yours, see, curved as a doe,
trust me. Though you have and I've broken it.
        Not the wrist. The trust. But
you know what I mean. In the distance, September
        burns maples into rubies and gold.
                If you follow
my wrist to my finger, you will see me
        pointing in a different direction toward a sky
                tossing and turning in diamonds.
This is the way
        I am going.
                Hold out your thumb
before I change my mind, before the road turns.

Leaving South Dakota

You are the lover who leans against the wall
between how it is and how it *is,*

you go to a strip club and spend
a year's worth of love

on flowers that darken
your lap

like our photographs, transformed
from silk and skin into something akin

to teeth marks on a windowsill, a bad habit
craving a complete breakdown.

The Badlands. The first time
you couldn't get it up.

I mean, we'd drunk six beers apiece
and run the Mazda up the muddy-rutted road,

its dirty sides steep, its middle high,
the car skidding and bottoming out—I'd never

felt so alive as on Sheep Mountain Table,
us rolling naked on a vacant hill,

the silent jags
ripped open, sunned and lightning-struck.

The mud-licked tires stayed mud-licked for months,
gray-clumped crusts falling off the rims

onto Kalamazoo streets for weeks,
long after those pretty western suns set.

I told you then I didn't care for the romance
of roses, preferred the simple

white and yellow of a daisy instead, a face
I could trust fully.

But every time your eyes glazed
like dead wings in winter and your body

rocked like a cradle in the kitchen and you fell
asleep in the light, the whole bedroom stunk

of juniper and lies. Always,
when the air feels like this

and the sky looks like it does, I feel drunk and high
on that hill, my heart a tizzy in love,

my head spinning, the sky setting
all around us red and hazy, the black birds,

whatever they are, circling and calling
from some strange gone world, far and low.

Embrace

If you're gonna fuck a stranger, don't do it
in Dubai. Unless you want to

spend three months in a penitentiary, that is, probably
without conjugal visits. In a NYC hotel, a bedbug

curves its hooked penis into a female and vibrates.
An Indiana house spider latches its teeth

into its mate. Behind a club in Vegas, two men
and a woman slam willingly against an alley wall, red feathers

sifting from her hair like angels.
It doesn't matter how you like it—

hard, soft, slow, fast, on your back or up the ass. Sometimes
life gives little choice. Take for instance, the moon

that day, still up from the night before. And that pink slip
she wore to open brunch, where her laughter was more

than enough to satisfy the hunger that wakes us all.
Hot coffee with fresh cream, mimosas, eggs the fluffiest thing

your tongue ever pressed, roasted red pepper smooth as saliva
sliding down your neck. Tiny French pastries so sweet

you can't pronounce their name. Her cheekbones
the color of strawberry, her face the only

planet, the only way to ever know a beach soft as starlight,
or flashlight catching you both pants down, slip up, before the authorities

pulled your bodies apart, cuffed your wrists,
hauled you off and locked you back in your own separate cells.

Failed Attempt

While sifting through a rack of jackets,
making room for summer, my hands
came across your hooded sweatshirt, stain
barely noticeable on the chest beside the zipper.
I thought of your bad heart. Pulled the door
which tends to stick sometimes to the floor,
walked out into the gentle rain straight to
the trash can, lifted its mouth. I heard yelling.
Felt you push my body. Remembered the holes
you made in the bedroom. I couldn't
give it away to Goodwill, that jacket, for fear
of bestowing negative energy pulsing your veins.
I thought of what you did to me: broken rib, split
lip. A line of rain drizzled down my arm and
I imagined you as a teen in your mother's kitchen
that one day, knife at your wrist, fountains of
thinned blood spraying the walls like pesticide.

Alarm

I'd rather wake to the crash of what could be
good mail splashing the living room floor.
To urges like hunger, thirst, or wanting
to make something beautiful. Thunder, poetry,

the smell of coffee and its dark cracking
to crumbs in the grinder's blade silver
and curved as the one strand of hair I found

on Valentine's Day one year
in a hotel bathroom in Sandpoint, Idaho.
I was 25 and pressed it between the pages
of a *National Geographic* without even thinking

of Elizabeth Bishop. My soon to be husband,
soon to be ex-husband and I
drove route 95's unstable lanes through February's
black ice, snow, and low visibility to feel

Ron Carter's bass thrum our skin.
We had argued earlier that morning
at a hotel where the heads of dead deer and moose
browned the lobby. We had fought

in the middle of night over the clicking clock
keeping me awake. He wouldn't sleep without an alarm.
It was the first time neighbors—no matter how temporary
—would call the cops.

Years later Jenny next door would tell me,
Once it was so quiet afterward
I thought he had killed you.
Our voices cut that Idaho night like a Tamarack

falling into its own shadow. A dark line
mistaken for horizon. All I wanted was to tuck that clock
beneath a pile of clothes—his black jeans, my woolen sweater.
The smallest peep, the tiniest cricket keeps me awake. But

he refused to pull that battery or even muffle the tick,
scared of sleeping too late. Scared of sleeping too late?
For what need we rise? It was too late already.
The muscles in my chest felt like a basket

of over-ripened tomatoes, my leaves wilting, my head sprouting
silver in moonlight, in the dark, in the morning,
behind the envelope of my right ear
trying so goddamn hard, for the life of us not to listen.

Transubstantiation

When I tell him
      I can't sleep
he tells me
      a story. Imagine
he says, a field

      ripe with strawberries.
and a dog
      made out of sponge cake
running through
      the field.

There is a whipped cream river
      and the dog, sopping
with sweet juice, black seeds
      on his belly, jumps in.
You take a spoon

      from your pocket
and eat him. You eat his paw.
      Eat his wet nose,
suck his tail like a line
      of licorice. He likes it.

He wants you to eat
      his soft body,
lick his sticky
      from your face.
You, too, want to feel him

    become you, feel his fur
brush your throat, crush
        his teeth with yours.
You've always wanted a dog.
        And now he fills

your veins, settles
        to the bottom
of your heart
        like small stones
in a stilled stream.

Advection, Nova Scotia

It floated in on the edge of our sight
like the ghosts of lost animals. We watched

it gather on the ocean, drift over white steeples,
red houses tiny as Monopoly pieces

on the peninsula below. We were eating
lunch on the peak of Mount Franey, a peach,

an apple, while it pushed its way up the peak.
On the trail, it closed us in

like puffs of smoke, like a bright moon
vaporizing. A strange bird

pecked at gray grasses. Everything had become
a shade of gray and we walked like shades

through these shades, the dark figures
of trees emerging like soldiers from white

fields, their rifles in their cradled arms shining.
We saw—we swore we saw—a pink shape

in the distance. An umbrella, a circle
of people looking down at a map. They pointed

at us and we pointed them in the direction
of the cliffs. That is where they needed to go.

A young boy dragged a stick leaving the forest
behind. Willows hovered rootless and we

floated beside each other, our gray faces and
dark eyes looking into what light remained.

Drops drizzled down my chin, down the insides
of my thighs. Our hands met and though they were

too wet to hold, we slipped into each other,
into white woods where we'd heard the calls

of moose, their bellows deep in our bellies,
wings from the grasses, their antlers rising.

Chico Hot Springs Saloon, Montana

I'm tempted to call it
Yellowstone's crown, how it sits
above the park, just after

sharpened roadside cliffs and wild
mountain sheep nibbling grass, a rustic
resort where women—young women,

the regulars, in pretty clothes sit
at high tables waiting
for men in cowboy boots to lift

their hands and guide them
to the dance floor.
The live band plays country,

the singer wears a silver cowboy hat
while the bassist, you can tell, wants
nothing but to play jazz.

The couples circle each other's bodies,
step with the music. It is so easy
to make up the story. One man

in tight blue jeans, sandy hair falling
far below his neckline, has a hard groove
and no form. He's the type of dancer

my father used to say would pull
a girl's arm from her socket.
He's all hip and swing, untempered

patter of boots. His partners dizzy
yet come back song after song for another
spin. One man, the gentleman, slightly

older, is a perfect square. His shoulders,
his hips, he holds the waist of his partner
like a strong wind. He looks into her

eyes and she glides anywhere
his motion takes her. And among
the girls, the middle-aged woman,

you can tell, gorgeous once, still
slim and energetic, laughing
in a leopard–skin-patterned shirt slipping

from her shoulder, claps her hands
to the music, slaps her thigh, dances alone
some songs, at the front of the floor.

Love,

       this moment will go.
This rain will lighten, the light
change, people will choose to wait
for things other than at these crosswalks,

things that come too soon,
others, they'll say, too late. Still,

the blinds in this booth, dusty
with conversation, raised just enough
for us to watch the wet streets darken,
our hands guiding smoke into our blood,

our skin pulsing with caffeine and hunger,
proves otherwise. Let the rain be the only thing

that moves, let it fall
like rain, bounce high

as that woman's thighs, her hand pressed hard
to keep her black hat back, let the rain

crash into traffic pulled off to the side,
and let the light

hold red, hold red, keep
the boy's eyes in the blue truck

looking up at the clouds, and the birds
beneath the awning dry. Let us stay

like this, you and I, the tips of our
fingers and every inch behind them
longing for more, the talk honest,
the laughter good. Again and again,

let the lives we do not yet know wait
for us, these bodies grateful and gravitating

toward the something we know not what
is here now, this moment, where

unexpectedly we've finally arrived.

Super String Theory, You Must Be Beautiful

Isaac and Albert, staring out their windows,
dreaming of apples and stars, sparked the wedding
of electricity and magnetism, rainstorms
and refrigerators, dodge ball and the atom
bomb, they opened the ache
to put tomătoes and tamătoes
in the same room together to discover
what makes them the same.
Super string theory, you must be beautiful.
Your silk bow shines like water around the waist
of the world. Surely, you must know, how is it possible
for the human mind to unravel
the mysteries of the universe, to unify
the basic principles of galactic life
when we cannot even acknowledge the basic
things that unify and make us us? Or is this only one
string? All across earth's landmasses, we
breathe and we die, we are loved or not loved
and we love or do not love back. Deep
in the seas, green strings of algae
also breathe. High on mountains, low in valleys,
along rivers, trees breathe, they remember,
they flinch at another plant's cut
stem. If it is possible that the sun and the moon and a
little rocky planet in a galaxy throbbing
with life plus lice on the raw skin of a dog and tumors
bulging in my grandmother's breasts, and a man's heart
breaking equals a series of numbers and letters, then
the answer seems to be written in a language
we do not yet understand. Einstein deduced

that if the sun disappeared, it would take
eight minutes for the earth to recognize the law
that says it's to spin out from its orbit's arms
and dance a new dance across space.
String theory, can you also deduce how long the ripple
will take to reach us when there are no more tigers
left in the wild, no Polar bears without cancer, no ice?
How long has it taken us to feel the disappearance
of the dodo? How long the loss
of God? What to do with the moon?
We lie to the world and send young bodies to kill
other young bodies on the other side of the world
we feel are not us. But surely, this must be
only one string, and on another, tell me
only peace vibrates. What's that wave like?
Not that there isn't something to tie us
to one another, to unify and justify
our behavior with that of black holes, not that there is
not a way to equalize both dark matter and light,
but why go so far to see what dangles in front of us
like an eyelash, like a dream luring us back.
Our lungs fill with air and the air with our breath.
When western man killed off most
Native Americans, the wave, according to the numbers,
turned a turtle onto its back and left it
heaving in the heat, praying in silence
for the sun to die, for the ripple to come.

Yaquina Bay, and Darkness

We have never been down this road: the ocean
a womb, if you can imagine that, and if you can't, just the ocean
pounding a March night black and blue, the lighthouse

at the end of the bay's arm beaming, ready,
metaphorically speaking, for delivery of
what we call the body

from what we call
the body—what we'll call here *our bodies*
from *our life together*—white glare, loose stone,
       the ocean—we fall into it all
blindly, everything—each word

that breaks free from our mouths, each word, that is, that breaks
our mouths, whether right or wrong, for richer or for poorer, each word
forming and forming and forming.

I fear this Pacific rising toward our feet and cringe at the sound
of the horn breaking night
with its wail, this night breaking us.

Every two minutes the horn calls the lost ashore, which feels like me,

which is surely us, out here
lost among tufts of beach grass like wild hair
over the world in which we've lost

the piece of driftwood we used to mark our path
back. Once, I halted, stilled my lungs
for the whisper I heard over my heart. I followed
the sound, sleeplessly, for days. So now

you know it's not good when I say let's stop
walking, let's sit on this log
in this fog, I could say, for as long as it takes to lift,

until the waves stop throwing themselves
against what we cannot see, that which we refuse

to see. I know I don't want to go any further.

Even Niagara Falls sounds like a sigh
from far enough away.

I don't want to go any further, I say.

You close your mouth—no, you, close your mouth, catch
whatever is left of us

not yet lost to this language.

II.

Song

We sat on flat gray rocks rising in rows
      like a choir. We held hands.
And when you leaned in to kiss me, like a mama
      bird you brought up into your throat
a cluster of fruit and cucumbers, dark green skin
      edging softer flesh and seeds.
This strange gesture you thought a symbol
      of love. Next time just bring me an apple,
I said, a handful of roses, a feather on a stick so I,
      too, can purge for you a song.

A Belly Full of Windows

In the room where I was born, the scent
of apples and blood. A cake

with blue-frosted windows.
Saline and faucet, nostril and pore,

my mother's drip. Out the autumn window,
who's to say? A gray day

on a New Jersey street, my crooked legs
already wanting to run, to walk out,
to leave her and her mother's Polish,

to climb out from the black mines
of her father and melt: a new moat,

the Atlantic shore. Or,

I was born in a garden, cucumber vines
twisting free. Could you smell me
over bumble and thorn? Were you there

when I was born? A bridge leapt a river
and I followed it

to my making, to my breaking.

First touch, then a wide red moon
swallowing my head, and always
thereafter, always a hand pulling me

toward earth. White plate, face, hands
hold my waist and raise me
toward, who's to say? White pine needles

called me toward her. Hands passed me
like bread until I felt something, my body
afloat, a boat across water. A hand

without finger or claw. Something
ungraspable, something with wings,
I am sure I remember

a little belly full of windows and questions,
heartbeats and clouds, mirrors and darkness,

darkness and thunder clapping and clapping.

Four Corners

There is a large man with a sled, splintered and wooden
        beneath its red paint's fading, selling roses
to the blind. Women passing in babushkas carry

        babka, paper bags, and milk. There is the rust of pennies
mixing with the scent of lemon candles, flames
        which must be shimmying like bellies

from the corner shop where the women know
        their sons go to purchase last minute gifts for their tables
where they lay breads and cakes and share words that take

        centuries to make, that take them back
to their mothers and fathers, back to their mothers, that take lifetimes
        and countries and tongues and songs and sex

and children to make. There is the presence of bees, hovering
        in a patient and stubborn cloud beside the stop sign
and a little girl in yellow hair ties wiping her runny nose on her older brother's

        even older sleeve. If you are one of the women, you cannot see her,
but hear her sniffling that, in a way, reminds you of cancer
        and tissues and pneumonia that never went away.

If you are the shop owner, you smell fruited clusters
        and imagine honey, both its aroma and its shade for the next holiday,
which is always approaching. If you are the man selling roses from your sled,

you do not understand what it means to be free,
yet do not mind being tethered to the idea of something
        blooming among thorns and beyond

its stem. Across the street, a woman stares at a moon flower
        opening in the florists' window until her eyes feel
they will break. Her eyes do not break, but instead fill with tears

        which she wipes discreetly with a blue handkerchief
she found in her mother's attic after she died. And like the girl
        in the hair ties whom she does not know and may never see again,

she is wet and leaking. She remembers shopping with her brother
        for candles for their mother's table long ago and hearing
how a bloom of honey bees will wait for their queen.

        How could they go on without her? At that moment, a blind man
walking past with a rose bumps her purse and does not
        apologize. The flower shop owner's youngest daughter

notices and thinks this rude. She squints her eyes
        and mutters something about a fat man selling roses
without a permit. When her grandmother—slicing bread

        in a busy corner of the kitchen, where steam from *stifado*
fogs windows and makes her stomach quake with desire, saliva
        moistening the corners of her mouth—overhears

her granddaughter, she yells something in Polish, her mouth
        mushing consonants into an angry porridge, which makes the girl
roll her eyes and walk away. In the center of the room, a dog lies

on a loomed carpet. A chewed rubber ball still at his front paws.
The girl kicks it as she passes. If you are the dog you keep on dreaming
        of fields green and blown by the breezes grasshoppers make

with their wings. If you are the grandmother, you're humming
        remembering the first time you and your husband discovered
the white flecks in each other's nails you named

        love clouds that come from touching each other's blind spots
in the dark. If you are the girl, you understand nothing of the humming
        waiting at the stop sign for direction. If you are

the woman, still pondering the moon flower, you decide to buy it and place it
        next to the green philodendron stretching and sunning itself
in the front window of your second story apartment, open and overlooking

        the intersection, so that little girl who passes every day
with her yellow hair ties will look up and think of the moon
        or of flowers.

Burial Grounds

Whoever finds us will think we were a small, stupid people.
Not small like Lucy with her pygmy horses and elephants, not small
like our cousin *Ardipithecus Ramidus*, Ardi for short,

whose bones surfaced near a lake in the Middle Awash, her hands
the same size as ours today despite her four-foot frame. Large hands
already predicting a future of Supermarket Sweeps, Supersize fries, Big

Oil, the Great Depressions. Hands shaped to take everything they want from
        the world
or raise men who will take everything they want from the world: hartebeests,
        river dolphins,
songbirds, bumblebees, gold, the simpler things that make us human

like starlight and sleep. Not small like Lucy or Ardi. Not small like my own hands
or my mother's who wears a size four wedding band and engagement ring.
Not small like my birth control pill. But rather, like the kid in elementary school

constantly spitting on children's shoes, the kid whose underpaid teachers say
he's old enough to know where and where not to spit. Like this kid's father
who smacks his son's head with his fist whenever he gets smart, this kid's feeble

vocabulary growing like a spider's web, catching quick, monosyllabic words
dad uses when he strikes mom. His father's words spider-egg sticky and growing
in this boy's mouth. Whoever finds us will find what doesn't decompose or easily

disappear. Things that leave traces, things that reproduce and resonate no matter
how much time and generations of man or ice pass. Mercury, radon, what we can't
        stop
ourselves from using—Styrofoam take-out boxes, batteries, cheap light bulbs,
and missiles—always so much to save. What fragments will remain

of our megachurches and temples? Wafer and paper, missal and kneeler, white collar, stained glass? Or, perhaps, a group of women and their broken vessels buried in lava four miles from a village where men waiting for water chewed khat and played cards?

Dig deeper: nuclear waste buried in containers of denial, bones of men who died mining for coal and salt. Giant lizards with feathers, ivory teeth, iron claw. All around them the earth pulsed, glaciers grew and receded, mountains sharpened like knives and dulled

like knives. What body will the earth randomly preserve that gives a slice of our long story to those asking to hear it again? Grave after grave of women, man hung on a plus sign around her neck, tiny diamond ring glittering like fairy dust on her small, left hand.

19-19

The game went into overtime that night. The moon didn't
Stay to witness, having other places to be. On top
Of Mount Thoradour she couldn't wait
To lose her virginity. This was before the war.
Before he would leave her

Pregnant with Sierra, alone, before he returned,
His left arm's ghost dangling from his side like a medal.
He was lucky, he'd tell her, her hair
Against his bruised cheek. The scent of her

Like orange groves for the first time again. This
Was before the dance where her little sister, who scored
The tying points in the game that night would break
Her ankle while dancing with George Thyman,
Her curious white bone pushing through the skin

Of this world before being forced back,
Sewn tight under the ivory-dry cast.
But this was before color. The black and white
The newspaper took still hangs on their father's wall.
Whenever Sierra sees the picture: her aunt's

Long caterpillar body balancing up toward the basket,
She remembers her mother pointing to the photograph saying
This was the night when the door to my womb unlocked.
When they married for Sierra, her sister came
On crutches with George Thyman. This was before

The last witch trial had taken place. In dense forests
Skirts still fanned cautiously around dark fires.
And this was before the reunion, before Sierra's
Mom would pull her blue Ford over to the side of the road
To wait out the storm. It was before the police would find her car

The next morning, empty, blood still wet on the steering wheel's rim,
Black windshield wipers broken, lying in the back seat.
This was when murder first entered the town of Pulaski.
The newspaper ran a story on the accident: Sierra's face
In color on the cover next to a reprint of her missing mother.

This was before the picture of her aunt that night on the basketball court
Would fade. That night on the court, ball rising from the arch of her
Fingers, circling the rim of the basket, wavering,
Then falling in, the whole world
Seemed right—she will remember this feeling
When she buries the ghost of her sister's body in an empty casket.

She will remember this as she buries her face
In her brother-in-law's empty sleeve, her niece embracing
The idea of the basketball
That made everything possible, everything feel
Secure. The way it fell through the chute, guided
By holes in the net. This was before the casket hit the ground.
This was before the war.

Miniature Museum, Prague

I pray for all
the faith we need

to carve Jesus' face
into a poppy seed.

To still our hands
enough to sketch

Elvis Presley
on a cherry pit.

I wish us
all the patience

it takes to hold still
as the artist who held still

during heartbeats,
moved between pulses,

to know our blood
deep enough to work

with and not against
its rhythm.

A caravan
of camels in a needle's

eye. A march of elephants
on a single strand

of human hair.
This is the body doing

what the body does.
What only the human

can do. In a nutshell,
a ship sails on

a mosquito's wing.
Clouds ripple downstream,

white pigeons in sunlight,
refection on reflection.

In a café, a man
cocooned in wires.

In a movie theatre, 1000
rounds in one vest pocket.

In a flea's hand, an hourglass
the size of a grain of sand.

On a tick's right wrist,
a watch clicks.

Gush

The toddlers almost get it, this chain-linked fence,
thousands of iron eyes replacing their mothers; the distraction

of castle captures them. They lift their legs, up
the wooden stairs they go clumsy like overweight soldiers.

They climb and they slide. The bird shit on the pillars shines
white as white on a magpie. Some pick at it like a scab

and flick it. Six children crossing a drawbridge
are six bridges crossing something drawn by man.

The sky is the color of bullets and the wood chips smell
like trees. *Slide, climb. Imagine wings.* Their mothers have

enough distance to wave now. Blood falls from the sky or, no,
it is cardinals fleeing. Imagine a sword. Its silver handle

encrusted with jade and mother of pearl, both for protection
and good luck. It is beautiful. A thin shaft of light

about to go out pulls a leaf from its stem.
Thousands of eyes follow the leaf to the ground

which trembles under the thunder which rolls
like a cannon ball through the children. The wind picks up

its sword and cuts the clouds open. The children
climb, slide, and drip, the cardinals wait in the trees,

puddles gather beneath the mothers, reflecting
the underside of umbrellas bursting from all the beauty.

Poem from the Coast

On the back of my sister's postcard I write *This
is what real starfish look like: fat and alive, yellow and purple.*

*When the sun opens, white specks on their arms shine
like stars in blackness; they are all your eyes desire.*

It wasn't until later, those fat purple starfish floating
behind my lids, that I realized I had said they *shine like stars.*

I hadn't connected their shine with their name.
At work, the sinks pile with dishes as I move

between tables. Drinks spill, drinks are poured, consumed
by drunks, and I carry their empty glasses

for cheap tips. At the end of the night, the eyes of minimum wage
cooks and dishwashers stare expectant as those children

years ago in Tijuana, holding out their hands
for salty watermelon, brown banana slices soggy as my paper plate,

their tongues starved for bad fruit that was, in their eyes, wine.
I think of the sea lion on the coast.

Not the small one curled in grass, a dead slice of shaded moon,
but its mother, a round hole

the size of a cantaloupe gaping from her neck.
And the crowd doesn't think it was a shark. The cut is too clean.

And we don't think rock, sharp and hidden in the deepening waters;
she would've known her world. And we don't think propeller. Surely

the sea lions would have swum from the boats. Day after day
the sun finds time between intervals of early spring rain

to dry and peel another layer of skin, the wind finds time to lift
and blow the pieces. The sea lion's skeleton starts to show, pointed bone

protruding through the nose, a white tulip rising.
And we stand and stare dumb, shading the great sun from our pupils,

hooded, and cowering against the rain wondering What did this?
What could it have been? What on earth broke her like this?

Fetus

You are so small.
One thump
in an infinite land of hail.

A white fungus of cells, a thimble
of flesh, a toe. Yet
already the body of a sand dollar, miles

and miles of our past curling toward your thumbprint.
You have slept within me since my mother's womb,
and now you have dropped.

What timing you have.
A war flashes against the clouds,
our coral, the ocean's

vibrant mind, dies one layer at a time.
Orca's eardrums explode from human noise.
Rivers are drying, we have little time

to dream. Oil coats the hollow bones
of Spanish doves. The salmon, even, are on their way
out. The moon has not the power it used to, the stars

are dark. This no place for you,
my child. You afloat
in this expanding universe,

it will collapse. You will be yanked out, cut loose,
wrapped immobile. And when they lay you in my arms,
you will have no choice but to come along.

Absolution

Chapter one: she contemplates, chooses. Chapter two: broken glass and flames, red clouds burning blue like blood on her doctor's smock the day before the appointment. Something has decided she has no choice but to have and name him. Chapter three: ripped tissue and stitches, her uterus bursts and is scooped out. Chapter four: her breasts wither. Chapter five: she raises him on Chapter six: baseball, burgers, and Chapter seven: bugs in jars. She kisses his head and he grows tall, likes girls. Chapter eight: he likes guns and ropes more than girls like him. Chapter nine. Chapter ten. Chapter eleven: one girl plus one rope plus one gun plus three bullets equals he's fifteen. Chapter twelve: someone decides he knew what he was doing. Chapter thirteen: Marshall sits still for his injection. Few protesters this time. Finally, rain. His mother lets it drip from her eyelashes and wishes she were chapter fourteen: the fertile earth taking him back.

Hunger

What feeds us is not the nipple.
It is the art of the nipple, its frame.

We take it all in, dousing the brain,
that mushy ruby

seduced by beauty, tricked
by spongy love.

We thought it was impossible,
but a tree crashed through a room

in our house and we were okay
with that. We burned it in the fire, the blaze

of life always burning. And the birds,
nesting, we saved their feathers

but burned them too. We ate their bodies.
We drank the ink

from the tree's berries and were finally able
to sing, to let the music

and language and grunts separate
from our bodies and decompose.

No, it is not the nipple that creates us,
it is the nipple that overfeeds us

until we run out of room in our attics
hovering like satellites over our heads.

Meanwhile, the grasses nod with assurance
and flick like wrists of conductors?

This is for you to decide. I put the mower in
the garage and pulled up a chair to watch

the wind shake the cold and fill its void
with more cold. I twisted my hair and bit

the tips of my fingers waiting to see what else
would come crashing down.

Revising the Body, Grand Teton National Park, WY

When I heard what he thought
was a plane, he and I were hiking.
For three miles we skirted the seam
between storm and sun, between
thunder and birdsong. Ask me

about love and I will tell you
about smoke. The occasional rings
hanging briefly in air, the air that splits
the circles open and pushes them
in directions they didn't know
they would go. The exhaling lover.
The inhaled other. The cravings.

The thunder. Behind us, gray swallowed
the Grand Tetons and cast off lightning.
Before us, billowing clouds plumed
toward sunset. He and I at the center, holding
hands on the shore of Two Oceans Lake.
Why do we promise for what will
speak, inevitably, for itself?

Rain cooled our sweaty bodies.
The meadow steamed. While my husband
in New York hovered between love
and distrust, our vows ringing out
of earshot, our circles rippling farther and farther
into that old unpredictable universe
whose stars we were not

afraid to name. Now, he and I walk blindly
through that same universe in complete
control. But I know better than that,
know the mountains that face us,
know other names for constellations that reveal
themselves only in dark, know I do not know
my own dark.

Love Poem Revisited

I love how we lay, a friendly stain
on a broken bed.

You keep your hand on my head.
Pull me closer than my husband ever did.

When you're not here, my fingers reinvent
your tongue. Wet sheets, wet pants
will dry. Oh, lovely impermanence.

You never asked why, but I have no tattoo
because touch is my tattoo.

Flesh pulled from flesh hurts
in all forms.

In the pillow, the smell of you
and my sheets are wet again.
I've never tasted come
so sweet. Soft as banana.

Once my husband made me come
so many times my hands I held
behind my head cramped on the tent pillow,
but I don't know if you want to know that.

It may not be true.
I might have been faking.

There is nothing that rots
like a marriage.

But I'll tell you, and I imagine you know
I'll keep this distance we insist but the other

night when you held me
because love is not enough,

when you touched my body over and over again,
when I asked like I do
if we could make love
and you said not tonight
like you do,

when you woke, sat up, and turned
to look at me
in a way you never have before,
the morning light red
through the curtain, I knew.

Love is not enough
remember

there is no one
only this distraction

attraction I guess it's called. We have
called it that.

But let's not name-call.
Let's keep on pretending it will never stop

raining, that the heart once broken
can never heal. Let's pretend misery has us
lying like this,

my whole body on yours, my lips on your lobe.
We sleep like this, you realize, me on top of you

and together we've dreamed of flying
over the world refusing the something
that can slide up into us

ten thousand times and have it
never be enough.

Picking Pumpkins

This time, just us, the only couple on the wagon
without children. We sit across from a baby

whose eyes are yet unfamiliar with this blurry earth
and its explosions—mums bursting from plastic pots, calves

galloping across a sunlit field. A pregnant woman
at the country store waves goodbye to her husband

who takes their boys to find the perfect pumpkin, some chapter
of the Cinderella story you never hear. The last time I did this

was with two girlfriends in Spokane. It was one of those
perfect fall days, cloudless, light illuminating the underside

of bright leaves. You could feel summer change
to fall on your skin. I could slow my thoughts enough

to notice such things then. This was before my heart
had learned to carry weight. To lift, like a dumbbell, marriage,

divorce, heartache, the sludge of depression up, down.
My grandmothers' hearts still beat, my grandfather's

cherry tree arched its dark branches over his garden.
It was a long time ago.

The three of us watched children chase chickens and caress
the long ears of ponies without the sight triggering

longing to have our own children. We twisted gourds
from vines and with a dull blade freed the fruit, keeping

large leaves intact, keeping it truthful. The way trees
should be drawn: leaf, branch, trunk, root down the full

length of the page. Our pumpkin vines were so long that day
we could wrap our lives in them. Now, he and I ride back

to the country store, the baby across from us holding
a tiny pumpkin in her lap, the smallest pumpkin on the wagon.

She fondles the trimmed stem as if it were a nipple. The only
thing in the world that makes sense to me, to my aging body

bumping over uneven ground and its dens, the animals inside
readying their young for winter.

III.

Before Fort Clatsop

There are shadows a flag casts, and places
that shadow does not reach. This stretch of beach,
kept sacred by winds and winter

and the hands that reach down to it,
discovers the waves by their crashing, the ice
by its cracking, the human voice by its wail

and song. This is a land of edges,
worn away stone. Here, we long
for that other shore that pulls like thread

through broken skin and sore muscle.
If we follow the river it takes us back
to a world of salmon and root.

If we stay we will be beaten by weather,
but there will be salt. What is it that leads us
always to the mouth?

It is so quiet I hear shells shake beneath my feet.
I wake from sleep and there is fur growing over my bones.
Lay your head on my shoulder.

Tomorrow we will all decide. For now,
we restless paw at each other, imagine dust
and sunlight and a land that echoes us back.

Separation in the Form of Fall

Today the dead drop from trees
like husks of heavy chestnuts.

Every time one falls, it frees another
to split open. I am not afraid

to be alone. I hear rustling
in the leaves, down they fall

through the light that leads out
of their bodies. They bounce and I hear

footsteps on my wooden stairs.
Once, I caught a walnut's loosening

and descent, watched it trickle and roll
through the leaves until it stopped

at my foot. I should've told you then,
should've cracked the husk open, placed it

on my tongue: husks are made for secrets.
I should've told you then.

We are always falling and splitting,
longing to free ourselves from those

we can no longer hold.

Pastoral

The old red tractor rusting to skeleton
by the fire pit. Stone wall crumbling

to flour on the property line. Pile of
wood, heap of splinter. All the grapes

have been picked by migrating birds,
their nests hang empty in trees

like hats. Windows so dusty
you can barely see in. But imagine

a bowl of blackberries
on that kitchen table, the adults

tuckered out from whiskey and wine, songs
and strings, dogs curled and sighing

in the pile of shoes on the floor, the children
asleep, the morning stars humming

behind their eyelids, the tomcat's muddy
paws tapping at the door.

The Courtyard

She appears from behind
a white pillar, a lamplighter
and I swear

small flames lift from her candles
like fireflies toward stars.
What she wears is not important.

She crosses the grass in the rain.
For hours I've watched puddles gush from the awning
of a monastery brewery. The bells won't stop ringing.

My blood lightens with pilsner
and the fried cheese and onions remind me
of my husband's breath, his nightmares, those spiders,

his screaming
for his mother from the center of our bed.
When I try to hold him and tell him

everything is okay, he flails, his body only
half-awake and therefore forgivable but still
I taste iron on my lips.

Once, we crossed a threshold:
he said *I hate you* and I knew I would never
let him take it back. Back then,

I'd rip my bitten nails down the runway of my neck
to feel anything but what we were doing to each other.
Scars and tissues,

smashed glass, stained walls,
the crescent moon dent in the bedroom door.
Those small white scars

on his hands like ghosts
from the year he washed dishes at the Bistro.
The stink of wet clothes in front of the basement fan.

If he were here right now
we'd be feeding each other olives, pretending to be in love.
We'd be talking Kafka in Czech, I'm certain, I might

lay my head on his shoulder, in that cove the size of a fist
he said I fit perfectly, I'd be ignoring the discomfort
that came with laughter and talk of kids, anything to do

with the body felt unnatural with him,
sharpened my heart into granite. Kids,
the ones we will never have,

the ones I could never imagine into being,
not in all those years our hands held each other's.
How I wish they could see the tree in this courtyard,

our little girls with their big brown eyes
and the rain sticking to the grass
like fire.

The Pianos Lay Down Their Bones

Tired of dissonance, the pianos
evolve. One by one, keys drop

to the floor and like magnets, the ivories
pull, the ebonies push toward the walls.

This is no war, no gang fight.
It is music.

Temperatures in their rooms climb,
shades lift, curtains sweep

open. In homes where pianos have stood
for years, cat paws in dust, grandparents' houses

where grandchildren sit on cold benches
running their fingers over keys, lace

unfurls, dry plants green. This is about rest,
about silence. The ivories spin into tubes,

into pillars and march toward the equator
where mounds of massacred elephants shake

like maracas and rise. The ebonies defying
gravity float upward, break

the atmosphere, and become the space
between stars. On clear nights

you can hear them tinkling, those tusked, gray
creatures below them, their giant

wrinkly bodies nestling with their families,
huddled in clusters toward sleep.

The Cardinal

It dropped into the mouth
       of a single sunlight tunnel, stood
alert, the only thing illumined in the garden.

I was reading Dante, his overgrown
sense of love, when the bird pulled me from my page. I

disappeared. How scaldingly beautiful, one blood red cell
in evening light. How powerful the body—what
muscular bird—frantic

       in high grass. Its head thrashed, its neck jerked
as if a dog, rabbit shuddering in its jaws.

 Last night, a leaf bug descended through moonlight
       and landed on the back of my hand. It
crawled into my palm and I lifted its eyes to my eye.

       It moved slowly, leafy wings iridescent like the inner life
of shells. I felt full and briefly believed

in the gods. In the grass, the cardinal
       lifted its beak. I could see the leaf-green wings.

I let it feed.

The Afterlife of Pennies

They become dollars.
Able to fold and no longer
in need of a train and its track
to bend. They lose
their weight, no longer a burden
to carry, and they learn quickly
how to use their newfound
silence, slipping
in and out of hands and pockets
with hardly any notice.
They begin, sometimes, to forget
the power in numbers.

For those at the bottom
of dark wells, the ground swallows
and returns them
through the mouths of volcanoes.
They become the earth and even
heaven's rain. The scales
shimmering on the backs of fish
and armadillos, noctilucae, the parts
of the moon that shine.

Some return
only through thought. Others,
when they've completed their journey,
when in this life they've taken less
and given more, it is believed
they become pure luck.

Meal

Today, we have warmed cups of Indian Ocean
infused with the curiosity of the woman
who first ate cardamom pods. An antipasto
of Tuscan grapes, Smoked Mountains, and
the sweet petals of earth's last orchids.
The soup is the perfect blend
of Georgian summer nights and the Perseides,
two pairs of eyes in two very different places
seeing the same star thread itself through the sky.
To cleanse the palette, a silver chalice
of Maine frost. A spoonful
of Antarctic evening, the sea-green sky wavering
within the ice. If you wish, you may dance.
The American Chestnut floor will be cleared
and wind will flow through the holes
of a Romanian flute and Shelley's
aeolian harp. Listen. Breath swirls through
a didgeridoo's pipe, hands beat a jimbe's skin.
As salt rises to our skin, we sip
a drought's first rain, and the first rain after
a long death. Refreshed for our main course,
do not expect it to topple the previous courses
or crown the remaining. All food is modesty
in a hand that feeds a mouth, all food is truth.
Your mouth will fill with bread shaped by
Afghanian women, potatoes plucked
by Irish men, mangoes growing
in Costa Rican children's dreams. The greens
taste like singing and fires on the Cape of Good Hope.
The beans remind of the womb, curled, waiting.

The coffee smells of Peru and tastes of all
who've ever loved you. You smile
and we again clear the floor. Only this time,
for weeping. And those who feel it can drop
the tears of every war, cry for unbreathed breath,
for every bullet blasted through a living body and into
the memory of a child not yet conceived.
For failed imagination's every stain.
We will follow the weeping with a long moment
of silence. Then, the song of the Bachman's warbler
will lift. We feel relief and satisfaction
and sit for dessert. A cherry pie
baked with Washington's fallen cherries,
Milton's apple pie, the seeds of Persephone's
pomegranate. After, crossing the wooden floor,
we will climb or descend the stairs
to where we will rest our bodies and minds,
and those other parts of ourselves
we still have not learned how to feed.

Fatness

                        He sweeps me off
to Venice anyway, buys me salt-water
taffy, warm eclairs in Rome, baklava
in Santorini, its ground fat and lumpy
with lava. When we scuba dive
through the gateways of an ancient city, pink
and purple coral glittering like dizziness
before our eyes, he squeezes my side and says
You're not fat. Enormous air bubbles fly
to the light. Even here my feet leave prints,
sand worms loop away from my body, a flounder
turns its head in disgust. Over croissants
outside the Louvre, chocolate mousse melting
down my frown on the train, over brie croquettes
on a tiny winery patio he says Quit your whining,
you skinny piece of love and I say I can't. I won't.
Everything we devour—even with our sight—even
with the cells of our skin that have already
touched each other and fallen away—how
I've draped myself in you. I am too full. Stop
loving me I yell. And he says Okay, I'm fat.
You're fat. We're all fat, bloated and floating
in the haze of this world. And I look at my knuckles
breaking the smooth curve of my fist, and at the hard
knobs of my knees, and at his eyes, how they hide
behind his lids. And I say No. We are not fat. We are thin,
too thin compared to the girth of the earth, to the weight
of the universe, and that our bodies are not large
enough to hold it all. And I say I am fat
but only because of love. And we agree.

Honeymoon

As we cruise the Mediterranean, I dream
every man I've ever loved. Every night I visit

each like he's is an island I docked for one night.
During the day, my new husband and I

encounter new languages on shore. Birds
we'd never before seen land near and sing us

their songs. People speak and we understand
little besides my warm belly under his soft hands, the sun's

heat, his neck beneath my lips, the tenderness of earth's
fragile creatures. Every morning I wake in a puddle

of sweat and drool, as usual. Every day I wake
in someone else's arms. All our lives together,

he must've unknowingly accepted from inside me
a piece of everyone I'd ever known, the many

slices of sweet cake returned to a whole. Still,
I didn't tell him what lay between my wet pillow

and dripping hair. How I turned away one lover's
mouth after another, ignored pleas, raised my left

hand to show them my ring, then unclasped a latch
at my chest saying, You need to go.

The Return

Fingertips that haven't touched
strings all summer, the hands

instead busy making unfamiliar
cheekbones familiar, loosening

braids to take home
the scent of linden. Like

a hummingbird's voice
hovering a lobe. Like tongue.

Like skin. His stroke
so holy it floats, this lingering

unafraid in the way
he hands everything back

to the world, so slowly as if
to erase the fact of taking

that is the world, the exchange
like a child's sleeping body

lifted from a car's backseat,
the small fist opened, draped

over a father's arm, the comforter
pulled back on the small bed, the body

slipped in like the long ride home
still purring under the tires.

ACKNOWLEDGEMENTS

I am blessed, lucky, grateful for so many wonderful people who have made this book (and life) possible. My mother and father who have encouraged and supported me in incalculable ways all these years. My sister Mirena, and the universe for making her my sister. Mom E and Dad E—a fountain of love and support—who together with my mom and dad have literally moved the earth for us.

I am indebted to my mentors-become-friends for so much good advice, coffee, beer: Nancy Eimers, Bill Heyen, Christopher Howell, Jonathan Johnson, Judith Kitchen, Tom Lux, Ann Marie Macari, Bill Olsen, and Stan Rubin. And the many gifted and generous writers I've turned to for feedback, especially Melanie Crow, Mike Dockins, Andrea England, Chris Vogt-Hennessy, Beth Marzoni, Susie Meserve, and Lauralee Pierce. You have all cared for my words as though they were your own, and for my experiences as though they matter. A special thank you to my cohort at the Inland Northwest Center for Writers MFA at EWU and our wine, cheese, and poetry nights, my fellow writers at WMU, and Gwen Tarbox, for lunch, for stories, for everything.

I am blessed to have found in my best friend and husband Rob Evory, the love, creativity, enthusiasm, adventurousness, positive energy, and good cooking that make our life one I am so thankful to live. I love and adore you.

Thank you to David Starkey and Chryss Yost for your work on this book and welcoming me into the Gunpowder family, and to Lee Herrick who in choosing this book as the winner of the 2018 Barry Spacks Poetry Prize made this possible.

ABOUT THE POET

Michelle Bonczek Evory is the author of three chapbooks—*The Art of the Nipple* (Orange Monkey Publishing), *Before Fort Clatsop* (Finishing Line Press), and *A Roadside Attempt at Attraction* (Celery City)—as well as the Open SUNY textbook *Naming the Unnamable: An Approach to Poetry for New Generations*. Her poetry is featured in the 2013 *Best New Poets Anthology* and has been published in over seventy journals and magazines, including *Crazyhorse*, *cream city review*, *Green Mountains Review*, *Orion Magazine*, and *The Progressive*. In 2015 she and her husband, poet Rob Evory, were the inaugural Artists in Residence at Gettysburg National Military Park. She holds an MFA from Eastern Washington University and a Ph.D. from Western Michigan University, where she currently teaches American literature. She mentors poets at The Poet's Billow (thepoetsbillow.com).

CPSIA information can be obtained
at www.ICGtesting.com
Printed in the USA
FSHW010639210319

9 780998 645841